FIELDS
of
GOLD

✢ ✢ ✢ ✢ ✢ ✢

A place beyond your deepest fears.
A prize beyond your wildest imagination.

ANDY STANLEY

A GENEROUS GIVING BOOK PUBLISHED BY

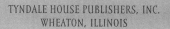

TYNDALE HOUSE PUBLISHERS, INC.
WHEATON, ILLINOIS

Visit Tyndale's exciting Web site at www.tyndale.com

Designed by Luke Daab

Library of Congress Cataloging-in-Publication Data

Stanley, Andy.
   Fields of gold : a place beyond your deepest fears. A prize beyond your wildest imagination. / Andy Stanley.
      p. cm.
   ISBN 0-8423-8540-1
   1. Christian giving. I. Title.
BV772.S72 2004
248'.6—dc22   2003022316

Printed in the United States of America.

09   08   07   06   05   04
 6   5   4   3

To my mom Anna Stanley,
the most generous woman I know

TABLE OF CONTENTS

INTRODUCTION

✤　✤　✤　✤　✤　✤

Giving was simple when I was a child. From an early age, I was taught to take one dime out of every dollar I received and put it in the offering plate. I never knew anything else. I was raised to believe that giving was just one of the things you did with money. It was effortless. And since I wasn't really earning the money anyway, I never felt any fear associated with giving. I certainly wasn't concerned that giving away money might be a threat to my quality of life. I always had plenty to eat and nice clothes to wear.

But over the years, as my income increased, I began to notice a slight hesitancy in my giving. I was still giving a dime out of every dollar. But now it was adding up to hundreds or thousands of dollars at a time. And somehow that felt different. Whenever I wrote one of those seemingly large checks, concerns such as these would run through my mind: *What if I need the money for something else? Am I saving enough? What if I have an unexpected expense? Is anybody else giving this much?*

My struggle didn't stop me from giving a set percentage, but it sure took some of the joy out of it. As I began to evaluate my hesitancy, I concluded that my problem wasn't greed. It was fear. I was slowly turning into a fearful giver. Bottom line—I was losing confidence in my long-held belief that God was who He said He is and that He would do what He's promised to do. Under the growing pressure to make ends meet each month, I was slowly becoming irrational in my thinking about God, His faithfulness, and my role as a steward of His resources.

Since that time, I've discovered that I'm not alone. For many believers, cheerful giving has become fearful giving. We are not opposed to supporting God's kingdom with our resources. And we're really not greedy. But we are concerned. We're concerned that if we don't look after our own needs first, they might not get looked after at all.

Yet the testimony of Scripture, together with the experiences of millions of believers, sends a resounding response to our concerns. Any fear associated with giving to God's kingdom is irrational. It's on a par with a farmer who, out of fear of losing his seed, refuses to plant his fields. As absurd as that may sound, many of us are guilty of hoarding the financial seed that God intends to be sown for the harvest that is to come. And it's all because of fear.

The principle of sowing and reaping applies to our finances. Those who sow generously can expect to reap generously and receive a bountiful return. Allowing our concerns about the future to limit our giving makes no sense at all. And yet, for many of us there is a lingering fear, a fear that has the potential to rob us of our joy. But worse than that, it's a fear that could cause us to handle our finances in a way that locks us in and locks God out.

In the pages that follow, we're going to unpack this irrational fear of giving. We will study the words of Jesus and we will peer into the lives of several of His modern-day followers. As we do, we'll discover that generous giving is actually an invitation for our heavenly Father to get involved in our finances. With His involvement comes a promise that should mitigate our fear of giving once and for all. He promises to resupply generous sowers with enough seed to continue sowing generously throughout their lifetimes.

The result?

Fields of gold—in this life, as well as in the life to come.

CHAPTER 1

DUST IN
THE WIND

✣ ✣ ✣ ✣ ✣ ✣

The western sky was growing dark. In a few moments, the entire Oklahoma panhandle would be engulfed in the swirling blackness. Jeremiah Clary began the familiar task of rolling up wet rags and stuffing them in the cracks around the door to keep the dust out. This particular afternoon, the churning winds were carrying tons of airborne topsoil in his direction. Even the slightest opening around a window would result in a solid layer of dirt on every surface in the house.

The Clary family had been lured to the Southern Plains by the promise of bountiful crops and endless, fertile fields of wheat. And for a while, that's exactly what they found.

But throughout the 1920s, thousands of ambitious immigrants plowed up vast portions of virgin grasslands to plant their fortunes. The Great Depression drove even more settlers westward, and they quickly exploited the organic gold mine of America's heartland. Then in 1931, the rains stopped. More than 100 million acres of hopes and dreams stood drying in the baking sun. But that was just a prelude to the real devastation. With nothing to hold the topsoil, the once benign winds of the western plains scooped up the loose earth one grain at a time and turned it into a giant sandblaster.

To make matters worse, the relentless sun radiated the exposed soil, turning the entire region into a vast clay oven that whipped the windstorms into an even greater fury. This unusual combination of earth, wind, and fire bore a resemblance to an apocalyptic wrath. Clouds of dirt rose miles into the sky, leveling everything in sight. Although it had taken a thousand years for an inch of rich topsoil to accumulate, it was blown away in a matter of minutes. In the wake of such a storm, fields of shoulder-high wheat were stripped bare. Tons of soil accumulated in drifts against fence lines, buildings, and dying livestock.

The drought would endure for a decade. As much as eight tons of soil per acre were lost every year. And all along, farmers like Jeremiah Clary kept thinking that surely the rains would return soon.

In a circular area touching five states, more than 850 million tons of land were lost. A reporter passing through the region described it as a giant "dust bowl." The name stuck.

Jeremiah lit an oil lamp as the whole Clary house vibrated under the onslaught of the black blizzard. Somewhere in the stratosphere above him was thirty-four dollars worth of Turkey Red, a special blend of seed he had sown the week before. It was headed in the direction of Missouri now.

Every time he sowed his fields, Jeremiah spent a month's salary in seed. And after five straight years with no income, it was getting to the point where he couldn't afford to keep up the routine much longer. He considered his odds of being wiped out again if he mustered the courage to replant.

Like countless farmers in his shoes, Jeremiah was battling an unusual form of anxiety. During the normal growing seasons of the wet years, it would have seemed senseless to stockpile seed during planting time. But under the strain of the times, many farmers were developing a psychological aversion to sowing. *What if another storm comes and blows away my investment . . . what if all my efforts get wiped out again . . . what if . . . what if . . . ?* Jeremiah began to feel a strange attachment to his remaining precious bags of seed. He knew they were worthless sitting in the barn. But Jeremiah couldn't help feeling that he was better off keeping them there, protecting them from the "what ifs" that blew across the plains with increasing predictability.

A few weeks passed, and some of the other farmers began to plant again. There weren't many days left before the window for germination would slam shut and another hot summer would be underway. Jeremiah almost trembled with indecision. If he didn't plant soon, he'd miss his chance for even a meager crop. And even a meager crop would at least replenish his stores of seed. But if he did plant, he could end up losing everything. He went back to the barn to check his seed one more time. The irony was overwhelming.

Jeremiah Clary was not a greedy man. But

under the mounting weight of uncertainty, he was slowly becoming irrational.

ABANDONING THE FIELDS OF GENEROSITY

You and I live in a dust bowl. Every day, we brace ourselves for the impending devastation that could sweep across the financial landscape and wipe out our stores of seed. In our world, the "what ifs" manifest themselves in circumstances such as diminishing retirement accounts, unexpected expenses, and worldwide economic turmoil. We stuff wet rags around the cracks in our portfolios and hope for the best.

In the midst of it all, we have a crop to produce—a spiritual crop. Like Jeremiah Clary, we have a limited supply of financial seed for sowing in God's kingdom. Perhaps you once dreamed of sowing fertile fields of generosity. But reality has taught you to be more cautious. *What if I give away too much? What if there's not enough left for me? What if . . . ?*

We're not greedy, but we are a lot like Jeremiah Clary. Under the mounting weight of uncertainty, it's easy to slowly become irrational about our possessions. We lose sight of who really owns them. We fail to grasp how we should be sowing them for God's kingdom. And we get confused about what we should really fear regarding our finances in this life—like facing eternity having sown only a few handfuls of our personal wealth for God's kingdom.

We're not alone. Millions of Christians around the world are frozen in their financial tracks by this anxiety. In all likelihood, they mean to be more generous. But somewhere along the way, uncertainty creeps in and they settle for the status quo: a watered-down version of what they could be sowing for God's kingdom—if it weren't for their fears.

In the United States, just one third to one half of all church members give any financial support to their churches. **Any.** And of the people who do give something, only 3 to 5 percent give a tenth of their incomes.

Meanwhile, the wealth accumulated by churchgoing people has reached record levels. And despite unprecedented opportunities for global ministry, American Christians give proportionately less today to the church than we did during the Great Depression.

Even those who do give are often tentative

and sheepish about it. They respond when the offering plate is passed or when the annual pledge cards are due. But there's not exactly a burning passion to leverage everything within their grasp to achieve God-sized missions. Too often, Christians take a posture that's reactive rather than proactive. People give reluctantly or to assuage their guilt.

For the most part, the church has responded by simply increasing the pressure on its members. Church leaders create clever fundraising campaigns, send out elaborate mailers, put big thermometers in front of the sanctuaries, and lock the doors until the goal is met. But beneath all this scrambling for market share, I think there's a root problem the church has mostly missed.

For many Christians, the problem isn't that the church lacks brand awareness. Nor is the problem that Christians are too greedy to give. For a lot of people, I think the lack of generosity among Christians can be attributed to plain old fear.

AFRAID TO SOW

Fear has always been one of the principal enemies of a growing faith. It has a way of clouding our thinking and obscuring the facts. You may know precisely how God would like you to handle your finances, but fear has the potential to freeze you in your tracks or send you down another path.

It's important to realize that fear and faith often go hand in hand. By nature, when you pursue a growing faith you increase your exposure to potential fears. Actually, fear and faith live parallel lives. Uncertainty is an essential ingredient for both. Without the element of the unknown, there could be no faith. It's in that moment of faith that we learn to rely less on what is seen and more on what is unseen. Faith bridges the gap. But it's also in that moment that we are most vulnerable to fear. Many Christians know how they'd like to give, but fear kicks in before they can bridge the gap with faith.

It's no accident that the Bible addresses this condition head-on. There's no drought when it comes to verses designed to help us let go of our fears and embrace our God-given calling to be generous stewards rather than fearful owners. In Matthew 6:33, Jesus assures us that when we seek His kingdom first with our seed, we need not fear being wiped out:

*... he will give you all you need from day to day
if you live for him and make the Kingdom of
God your primary concern.* (NLT)

As we are about to discover later in this
book, God's nature is to replenish the stores
of those who strive to be faithful conduits
for His kingdom work. When you participate
with God in His mission, you can trust Him
to reward you abundantly for every good
deed. When you begin to view your wealth
from God's perspective, you'll see that the
thing to fear isn't giving away too much, but
sowing too little.

CHAPTER 2

A GROWING AMBITION

As a pastor, my primary responsibility is to encourage and equip people to grow in their relationship with their heavenly Father. In fact, the mission of North Point Community Church is to lead people into a growing relationship with Jesus Christ. But there is also another arena in which I am responsible to help people grow: financial stewardship. As believers, we all have a responsibility to leverage our wealth for kingdom purposes.

I rarely encounter resistance when I talk to people about investing in their relationship with an invisible God who loves them unconditionally. But the brake lights often come on when I urge people to give their hard-earned money. The "what ifs" shower down on them like a spring rain, dousing whatever spark of enthusiasm I am able to kindle.

I realize that the fact that I am a pastor may give you reason to suspect my motives. It could very well be that you have had a bad experience with a pastor somewhere along the way. Worse, you may have had a bad experience with a pastor that involved your money. The good news is that I don't want your money. You won't find an envelope with my church address taped in the back of this book.

Furthermore, this is not a book about tithing to your local church. My goal in writing this book is to free you from a percentage mentality and to introduce you to a way of life built on the premise that God is a rewarder of those who seek Him and His kingdom first. Once those two truths become front and center in your thinking, your fear of giving will dissipate. Then, and only then, will you be free to experience the thrill of fearless giving.

BORN TO GIVE

I wish every Christian were as fearless as Milton Scott. He gave about as fearlessly as anyone I've ever known. For the most part, "Mr. Milton" blended quietly into the landscape where I grew up. But beneath the surface, his story had the makings of folklore.

By the time he died at the age of 106, Milton Scott had experienced more of life than ten average men. Born in 1895, he lived in three different centuries. He saw a demonstration by the Wright brothers with their first airplane. He attended a parade for Admiral Dewey, hero of the Spanish-American War. He commanded a U.S. unit of black soldiers during World War I and was given the French Legion of Honor, France's highest national award. He had a loving wife and four daughters. He took daily walks throughout old age, and when confronted one evening by a mugger with a gun, he told the thug to go ahead and shoot because he didn't intend to cooperate. (The mugger fled.) During his lifetime, he watched transportation advance from horse and buggy to the space shuttle.

In business, Mr. Milton also had his share of opportunities. As a young man, he became related to Atlanta's Candler family by the marriages of two Scott sisters to two Candler brothers. Mr. Milton looked on unimpressed while investors were sought for the marketing and distribution of a new drink Asa Candler was marketing. Whenever he told the story later in life, he would shrug casually and explain, "I didn't want none of Asa Candler's Coca-Cola."

Milton Scott had his own life to live. He operated a successful textile mill from age 25 until he was 102, when he sold the company to a British conglomerate. Even when he was no longer involved in the day-to-day operations of the business, he prayed regularly for the company.

Perhaps the most remarkable thing about Mr. Milton was how uncompromising he was about his kingdom calling. He was born to give. More specifically, he felt called to put God's Word in the hands of people who were eager to absorb it. And he knew no greater joy than finding a new Bible distribution opportunity to fund; he called these distributions his "projects."

For himself, Mr. Milton allotted a very meager lifestyle. He typically kept four suits, four pairs of shoes, and half a dozen white shirts in his closet. He drove a basic American car, replacing it every ten years. He lived out his days in the same house he had built for his bride in 1920. No modern kitchen. No Jacuzzi tub. He didn't even have air-conditioning until he was in his nineties, when a live-in nurse required a window unit to stay comfortable.

On a typical day, Mr. Milton would eat a bacon breakfast and then sit in his favorite chair reading the Bible for one or two hours. On average, he would read through the entire Bible four or five times per year, a pace he maintained for eighty years. After Bible reading, he took the short ride to work where he tended the mill and his prayer closet. He enjoyed hamburgers, Georgia Bulldog football, and telling jokes. Masterfully, he balanced simple living with a zest for life.

Unlike most people with a growing income, Mr. Milton didn't elevate his lifestyle in turn. Nor did he fumble for a twenty-dollar bill when the offering plate was passed. For Milton Scott, funding the work of ministry was a priority. And fund he did. In vigilant secrecy, he went about the task of dividing his sizeable earnings among God's interests around the world. Along the way, he amassed a list of accomplishments many charities only dream about.

He helped to smuggle thousands of Bibles

into Russia before the Iron Curtain fell. He single-handedly funded a ministry that equipped lay preachers across South America. By himself, he was one of the largest sources of aid to the country of Bangladesh for two years in a row. He was personally responsible for the printing and distribution of more than thirty Wycliffe Bible translations. In China, Egypt, India, Central America, and countless other places, innumerable people got their first glimpse of Scripture because of his vision and generosity. He also took literally the call to care for widows and orphans, supporting a widow ministry and paying the college tuition for several children of deceased parents.

Mr. Milton sent his assistants to investigate the inner workings of the ministries he was considering helping. As soon as God placed a suitable project on his desk and the money in his account, he would get to the task of giving. It was not uncommon for him to clean out his account two or three times a year. In his later years, a nephew in charge of his estate would often have to notify him when the money had run out. Whenever his account was replenished again, his giving would resume.

Mr. Milton seemed impervious to the "what ifs" most of us fear. Not that they weren't familiar. He had lived through the Great War. He survived the Great Depression. He raised a large family. But despite all those invitations to worry about himself, he was much too enraptured in the joy of giving to notice. He didn't amass a reserve fund. He didn't watch the stock market. He just gave and gave.

Because of his commitment to secrecy during his lifetime, no one knows exactly how many millions passed through his hands. Conservative estimates suggest he gave at least 70 to 80 percent of his income. At least. And all along, he maintained a lifestyle that barely qualified as middle-class.

FINDING YOUR GIVING THRESHOLD

Milton Scott's story has a way of putting things in perspective. It should make us think twice before casually throwing around words like *generous* and *self-sacrificing*. Some considered him extreme, but we can all agree that he took giving very seriously.

Now before we go any further, let's get personal.

When you were reading Milton Scott's

story, did you think about your own giving a little bit? Did you feel challenged? Convicted? Depressed?

I'll ask you the same question I ask myself. If Milton Scott can live in the South with no air conditioner while giving away the majority of his income, what's a reasonable amount to give away during our lifetime?

Would you consider giving 50 percent off the top for kingdom work?

Okay, so maybe that's a little high. But surely, 30 to 40 percent off the top sounds reasonable, doesn't it? I mean, you could probably still afford luxuries such as air-conditioning at that level.

How about 20 percent?

10 percent?

Now I have a confession to make. My whole purpose in telling you the Milton Scott story was to test you. And the challenge I just issued was also part of that test. So let's see how you did.

For most of us, the idea of giving away outlandish portions of our money elicits a sense of fear. When challenged with the idea of giving more, what kinds of feelings did you experience? Maybe it caused you to entertain some ways to increase your giving:

some sacrifices to make or possibly some lifestyle changes to consider. Were there any signs of fear?

Here's a scary thought: *What if God called you to give beyond your comfort level?* Would you be afraid? Would you try to explain it away or dismiss it as impractical? And in the process, would you miss out on a harvest opportunity for which God had explicitly prospered you in the first place?

You see, when we respond in fear to an invitation from God, we forfeit the reward of being faithful stewards. Sowing in faith results in an eternal crop. Cowering in fear yields empty fields.

Over time we get so used to rationalizing our way around those challenges that we just grow numb to them. When that happens, it's easy to discount stories like Milton Scott's as unattainable (or impossible) extremes. We toss them into the same category as Mother Teresa, the apostle Paul, and dozens of other examples we feel we'll never live up to. We admire those courageous men and women, but surely we're not intended to be like them. Right?

Before you pass over this one, think about how the idea of giving more made you feel.

Were you uncomfortable? Were you afraid? What kinds of thoughts went through your mind as I challenged you with those percentages? Did you start a list of reasons why you can't give beyond a certain point? Did any "what-ifs" come to mind?

Everyone has a threshold when it comes to giving. Whether it's a dollar amount or a percentage, there are some giving levels that are effortless and others that make us uneasy. No matter how far you're willing to go for God's kingdom, sooner or later you hit a wall. For many Christians, the wall is fear. Until you recognize it, you'll never be able to break through it.

By nature, the concept of generosity is in direct conflict with the concept of self-preservation. There's a point at which your own generosity will pose a direct threat to your well-being. Conventional wisdom tells you that unless something governs your generosity, you will give your way right into the poor house. The potential of not having enough is a reality for everyone. So it's only natural to feel torn between the desire to share with others and the desire to protect yourselves. Your heart wants to be generous, but your emotions register fear.

When you became a Christian, you signed up for a completely different economic system. Whether you realize it or not, identifying with Christ entitles you to a very special compensation plan. So while the world around you perpetuates the idea of looking out for number one, Christ calls you instead to look out for the interests of others. In fact, He promises to take care of you while you do.

This means that when a Christian reaches his giving threshold, he has options the non-Christian doesn't. The non-Christian must stop. If he doesn't look out for himself, perhaps no one will. But as a Christian, you don't need to be limited to a threshold of fear and self-preservation. The limits for your generosity aren't prescribed by mere financial principles. And often, stepping outside your comfort zone is not careless irresponsibility, but a necessary act of obedience.

It's natural to feel afraid when you begin to give outside your comfort zone. You may begin to second-guess your generosity. Even if God gives you an obvious opportunity to give, it's not always easy to do so. And if you're not prepared for that moment, your fear can hinder your ability to be a good steward of God's resources.

In fact, of all the things that keep Christians from stepping out of their comfort zone, fear may be the most significant. Sure, greed plays a part. But I think more times than not we simply "what if" ourselves out of giving the way we'd like to. *What if the economy falls apart?* Or *What if I lose my job? What if another war breaks out? What if I have an unexpected expense? What if I can't pay my bills?*

Over time, you can grow accustomed to explaining away your opportunities to give. Your heart can become numb to the needs around you, needs that God intends for you to meet. And it all starts with fear.

DISMANTLING FEAR

As a pastor, I see two kinds of givers: people who give what's left over, and people who give off the top and live on what's left over.

The first group isn't greedy. They just operate by different priorities. They see themselves as responsible for meeting their own needs. And whatever's left over goes to helping God's work. Do you know anyone like that?

The second group sees everything as belonging to God, including the responsibility to meet their daily needs. Therefore they're free to take on the mission of stewarding God's resources as their generosity dictates. Generosity is their priority, although they don't give carelessly. They give thoughtfully and effortlessly.

The problem with giving leftovers is that your generosity can never exceed your ability to meet your own needs. If you prosper, there may be some left over. But the minute you face financial uncertainty, generosity takes a backseat.

In 2 Corinthians 9:7, the apostle Paul says, "Each man should give what he has decided in his heart to give, not reluctantly or under compulsion, for God loves a cheerful giver." God intends for us to give out of a cheerful heart. But the more your heart is occupied with the burden of meeting your own needs, the less it can entertain God's promptings to be generous.

For the people in that second group, the generous givers, giving off the top is only logical. They understand that God owns and controls it all. They feel free to invest in His interests first and their own needs second. It's the rational thing to do.

For leftover givers, it's always a struggle

to let go in this area. They've heard the sermons. They've read the verses. They've listened to the testimonies. But somehow, they still hold back. They have families to feed, retirements to fund, and markets to second-guess. So they hold back on God, afraid they can't manage all their financial responsibilities and give to God's work too.

A little fear can be healthy, but it can also be dangerous. It has the power to make you act contrary to your beliefs. In essence, it can make you irrational.

Isn't it rational to trust God with your finances, since all of it belongs to Him? And isn't it rational to trust God with something that's beyond your control anyway? Therefore, doesn't that make it *irrational* to trust God for your eternal destiny, yet decline His invitation to direct your finances?

Fear has a way of twisting the truth.

THE MOMENT OF TRUTH

As you move forward in your relationship with God, occasionally He will test your grip on your wallet. It's a faith thing. It doesn't happen every week or every month. But every so often, God will prompt you to step out of your generosity comfort zone. And if you really want to keep God in control of your finances, you need to follow. There's a line you must be willing to cross. You must be willing to go where you can't rely on your own financial stockpiling, but only on the Lord Himself as your provider. I'm not talking about acting irresponsibly with your money. I'm talking about an attitude in which God's voice is louder than the soundtrack of "what ifs" in your life.

You can think of that line as the "what if" line. You'll know you're getting close to it when your desire to follow your generosity is met by thoughts like, *What if the interest rates change?* or *What if inflation picks up?*

Like we said, that line is different for everybody. For example, 10 percent has always been pretty easy for me. I was taught to give a tithe with my very first allowance as a kid. So that's never been much of a struggle. For me, tithing is well within my comfort zone. I could tithe my whole life without getting close to the fear threshold or truly dealing with the issue of who owns my possessions and who provides for my daily needs. But throughout my life, there have been defining moments when I was challenged to go above and beyond my regular giving. And each time I faced one of those challenges, I experienced fear.

Fear is a regular part of the landscape for anyone who wants to grow in faith. There's always a trace of nervous energy when you stand near the edge. In that moment of uncertainty, when you place your financial future in the hands of an invisible God, it's only natural to feel butterflies.

Even when we've prepared our hearts to hear the Holy Spirit's promptings, obedience is not always easy. The first time I was challenged to give above and beyond, I was a junior in high school. At a Sunday night church service, a young nursing-school student came forward to share a prayer request with my dad, the pastor. After the inaudible interchange, my dad suddenly spoke up over the music. Even though it was out of the ordinary for a Sunday night service, God had put it on my father's heart to share her situation out loud. She needed money for nursing-school tuition.

As soon as my dad explained her story, I felt an internal nudge that I should give her one hundred dollars.

That may not sound like such a big deal today. But to a high school student in 1975, it was a lot. I was making $2.90 an hour cleaning the meat department at the local Winn-Dixie, trying to save up for a car. Not to mention, I was already tithing on that. So the idea of parting with a hundred dollars in one generous act was like jumping off a cliff.

The tension was powerful. On one hand, I wanted to be generous. But on the other hand, I was afraid.

At first I tried to tell myself I was just having a "generous moment." Do you know what a generous moment is? It's the way you feel when you hear stories of starving people in Africa or homeless children in the inner city halfway across the country. Most generous moments aren't very threatening. The financial need is usually so far away that it's obvious you aren't meant to be part of the solution. It's safe to feel a little compassion without endangering your own quality of life.

But this generous moment was standing right in front of me. And it was about to set me back a month's pay. The "what-ifs" were filling my mind faster than I could process them. *What if I never get that car? What if I need the money for something else? What if I change my mind later? What if I'm just being emotional?*

There was something so right and purposeful about the idea of giving her the money. I felt sure God wanted me to do it. But at the same time, there was something very real about my fears.

In the end, I gave her the money. The fear never completely went away. But for whatever reason, I resolved to take all my fears and say, "God, I don't want to be impulsive, but I don't want to let fear get in the way of following Your will when You prompt my heart. I'm not 100 percent comfortable giving this money, but I'm too uncomfortable not to give it."

I don't know if my hundred dollars made the difference for that nursing student or not. But I do know that it made a big difference for me. That moment of trusting God in the face of financial fear has been a model I've gone back to over and over as I've followed God in progressive stewardship over the years. It was a defining moment in my faith. I can't recall anything else I spent a hundred dollars on in high school. I certainly don't have anything to show for the other money I spent. But I'll never forget surrendering to God's prompting to give.

FEAR FACTOR

If you experiment with generosity long enough, sooner or later you'll come face to face with fear. As frightening as it might feel at times, God gives us financial seed for one purpose: sowing. Unless we open our palms and let the seed fly, we will never know what fruit He might bring from it.

I don't know how Milton Scott dealt with fear. But from my experience, I know it's a constant test of faith to live with an open hand financially, giving freely, and trusting God to replenish your stores of seed.

Throughout my life, as I've wrestled with the desire to open my hand, I've discovered that I'm not alone. I've talked to hundreds of people who also want to make a difference with their possessions. Like me, they're all wondering the same thing: *How can I get in on what God is up to financially in the world? And how much will it really cost me to do so?* The struggle between fear and generosity is so real you can almost see the internal wrestling match.

The solution to this tension lies in changing our idea of ownership. Who really owns your possessions? And who's calling the shots for you financially? If you believe that everything truly belongs to God, then you have nothing to fear after all. And if God is the source of all wealth and He controls the comings and goings of your money, then there's no reason *not* to give.

But getting God involved in your finances involves surrendering control of your money to Him. And it means answering the call to generosity. To the degree that you surrender control, you leave fear behind and experience the kind of generosity God intends. In fact, Jesus' model for generous giving was a widow who gave her last penny (see Mark 12:42-44). She had nothing else to rely on but the promise of God to meet her needs. Frankly, I'd be a whole lot more comfortable if stories like that hadn't made the final draft of the Gospels. It takes courage just to slow down long enough to let their meaning sink in. But when you do, there's little room for misinterpretation. God doesn't want our generosity to be limited by fear.

In every person's life, God plants the question: "Do you trust Me?" To trust in Him financially means we experience peace and contentment while we enjoy the thrill of participating in His financial mission for the world. To trust in our savings account means we experience anxiety and anguish while we miss out on one of life's central invitations.

The danger of not crossing the line, wherever it is for you, is that you leave God out of your finances. Saying no to God in this area is tantamount to telling Him you don't want Him involved when it comes to matters of your possessions—and ultimately, your heart.

Maybe God hasn't called you to give at the level of a Milton Scott. But has He ever prompted you to a level of generosity that felt a little uncomfortable? Has fear ever kept you from following Him and doing something financially for His kingdom? Is it possible that you could get to the end of your life and never know for sure?

Spend some time praying over where that line is for you. But if you really want to move beyond your fear, to experience the unbridled joy of generosity, brace yourself for a principle and a promise that could change your life forever.

CHAPTER 3

TRADING
PLACES

✢ ✢ ✢ ✢ ✢ ✢

Billy Ray Valentine got a crash course in stewardship. He was the fictitious street beggar in the film *Trading Places* who experienced an overnight reversal of misfortune. Millionaire brothers Randolph and Mortimer Duke theorized that they could take an underprivileged hoodlum like Billy Ray and transform him into a productive part of their investment empire. They gave him new clothes, a new home, a chauffer-driven limousine, a butler, and a prestigious position at their firm.

At first, Billy Ray didn't get it. When the Duke brothers gave him a tour of his lavish new townhouse in uptown Philadelphia,

Billy Ray was covertly stuffing his pockets with anything that wasn't nailed down. Randolph tried to explain that the whole place belonged to him now. But Billy Ray saw the situation through a different lens. He came from a world of financial fear. He was afraid if he didn't seize the opportunity to meet his own needs, he might go hungry. And the Duke brothers' explanations of pork bellies and commodities futures went right over his head. So Billy Ray was focused on whatever loot he could get his hands on: Cuban cigars, fistfuls of chocolates, and gold-plated trinkets that could be traded at the local pawn shop. It was the only way he knew how to operate.

Eventually, Billy Ray caught on. He began to trust what the Dukes were saying and he realized that he no longer had to fear hunger. Before long, he began to shift his focus away from his basic needs and onto the task of managing the affairs of Duke and Duke. Once his perspective changed, he actually became a valuable employee.

I can't help thinking that many Christians are a lot like Billy Ray Valentine. God wants to entrust vast portions of His empire into our care. Not for our personal consumption, but to be sown for His kingdom work. He wants capable managers to handle His affairs, distribute His wealth, and spread His message.

But do we really get it?

The statistics about our giving levels suggest we don't. We're surrounded by God's vast riches and His lavish promises to meet all our needs. He has given us a simple task: to be good stewards of His resources, leveraging His wealth for kingdom gains. But somehow, that seems to go right over our heads. Just like Billy Ray Valentine, we often stuff our pockets with every penny of surplus God gives us. We come from a world where poverty is only a pink slip and a few bad investments away. We've learned to be fearful. Too often, we're more concerned about our next meal, or the mortgage, or our 401(k) than we are about investing in the Kingdom. So whenever God blesses us with more than we need, we see it as an opportunity to insure our future or to guarantee our next meal, while all along, God meant it as an opportunity for us to give more.

Along the way, generosity often gets demoted to an afterthought. Instead of being our job description, it's something we think about only when we have leftovers. Our generosity becomes limited by the amount of surplus we've amassed at any given moment. That's a picture of cautious generosity, a generosity that's been ravaged by fear.

The concept of fearless giving might be new to you, but it's been around for a long time. One of the best examples of generosity comes from a local church in the first century.

THE LAW OF THE HARVEST

In his second letter to Christians in Corinth, Paul commends them for their generosity to believers in another city.

But sensing the natural tension between generosity and fear, Paul took the opportunity to bolster their confidence by reminding them of the terms of their new position as managers in God's kingdom. In the process, he gives us valuable insight into the new relationship between our needs, the needs of those around us, and the God whose mission it is to meet both.

This passage is crucial to your understanding of God's response to your giving. It offers a behind-the-scenes look into the world of your heavenly Father. It underscores what

He's up to in your world, and how He wants you to participate with Him.

> *Remember this: Whoever sows sparingly will also reap sparingly, and whoever sows generously will also reap generously. Each man should give what he has decided in his heart to give, not reluctantly or under compulsion, for God loves a cheerful giver. And God is able to make all grace abound to you, so that in all things at all times, having all that you need, you will abound in every good work. As it is written: "He has scattered abroad his gifts to the poor; his righteousness endures forever."*
>
> *Now he who supplies seed to the sower and bread for food will also supply and increase your store of seed and will enlarge the harvest of your righteousness. You will be made rich in every way so that you can be generous on every occasion, and through us your generosity will result in thanksgiving to God.*
>
> (2 CORINTHIANS 9:6-11)

This passage shows us three key insights that can help us understand what God desires from us in the area of financial giving and why our fears are unfounded.

INSIGHT 1—THE LAW OF THE HARVEST APPLIES TO YOUR FINANCES

". . . whoever sows generously will also reap generously . . ."

The first insight Paul reveals is that the law of the harvest, the principle of sowing and reaping, applies to your giving. This simple observation can revolutionize your perspective on generosity. In essence, Paul is saying that those who give generously will receive something back in return for participating. Furthermore, there's a direct correlation between how much you give and how much you get back. The more you sow, the more you will reap. It feels a little risky to say this, but I believe Paul is actually suggesting that the amount entrusted to you in your life often depends on how well you steward what you've already got. If you give like you're supposed to, God will give you more.

Now let's face it. This principle has been taken to all kinds of extremes. Some people have misused this passage for personal gain. All kinds of wacky promises have been offered: "Send me a dollar and God will give you ten in return." And a lot of people have been disappointed because they expected this principle to make them rich.

Paul wasn't talking to people who were trying to get rich. And he wasn't trying to get their money. Paul already had it. He was simply explaining how God wants faithful men and women to act as conduits for distributing His wealth around the world. Not for personal gain, but for kingdom progress. Paul was offering encouragement to those who wanted to move beyond their fear of giving and cross the line to unbridled generosity. He wants us to know that it's safe to obey God and to be good stewards.

This is good news for reluctant givers. When you give away something valuable, it feels like a loss. You had something. Now you don't. And that can be a tremendous disincentive to give more. But Paul puts this concept in a completely different light. He says that giving to God's work is not giving something away. It's an investment, not a loss. The farmer who sows doesn't lose seed. He gains a crop.

What rational farmer would say, "I'm afraid to sow my seed because then I won't have the seed anymore? What will happen if I need this seed?" Any farmer knows that if he wants a crop, he's got to sow his seed. It doesn't benefit him to stuff his pockets full. Neither does it do any good to pray, *Oh, God, please give me a crop. I'm not sure I'm ready to sow any seed, but God I'm trusting You to get involved. And I'm holding onto my seed just in case.*

This is powerful news for anyone who's afraid to give because of financial insecurity. It suggests that the wisest move we could make financially is to begin sowing our financial seed. When we do, God gets involved in our finances. And that's the most financially secure place we could be. If you've never been a bountiful giver, chances are you've never seen this work in your life. It's no wonder you might be unsure.

But Paul tells us that anyone who is willing to sow handfuls of seed can expect an appropriate crop in return. It's a principle. When we give, it enables God to return to us more than we've given, to entrust more to us in this life. Which, in turn, enables us to give more. And round and round it goes.

INSIGHT 2—FINANCIAL GIVING ALIGNS YOUR LIFE WITH GOD'S AGENDA

... He has scattered abroad his gifts to the poor;
his righteousness endures forever ...

It's one thing to give because it makes us feel good or because we'll have God on our side financially. Those are admirable motivations. But there's another reason that's even more fulfilling than either of those. Paul touches on it in 2 Corinthians through an obscure reference to Psalm 112.

He has scattered abroad his gifts to the poor;
his righteousness endures forever.

At first glance you may be wondering, *Why did Paul put that in there? What's that got to do with anything?* Scholars have their various viewpoints about Paul's intended meaning. But without getting into deep analysis, there's a basic takeaway that we can get from this passage. Paul is reminding the Corinthians of God's commitment to disperse His gifts and care for the poor. In other words, God is up to something in this world. And when we get involved with Him this way, we are taking our place in a plan that's much bigger than our life and our little bucket of seed. We are participating in God's providential plan for the world.

God is concerned about the poor, and He's concerned about the Great Commission. That's what He's about. He's made a promise to care for poor people, and He's promised that the world is going to be evangelized. And He's committed to those objectives. But they're going to cost money. The fact is, God will get the money from somewhere, but He'd rather partner with His people to accomplish the work. He's looking for people who are trustworthy stewards to participate with Him by voluntarily using some of their finances in order to fund His interests.

So what do we have to fear? Why in the world would God drain you of your resources and then not replenish them to accomplish what He's committed to doing? In other words, if you are a partner with God in this, why would He hinder your ability to give toward the things that are the passions of His heart: the poor and His ministry?

God is going to do it with us or without us. But He invites us to partner with Him. And when we do, our lives take on a whole new level of significance.

INSIGHT 3—GOOD SERVICE RESULTS IN REPEAT BUSINESS

. . . You will be made rich in every way so that you can be generous on every occasion . . .

Finally, Paul makes a rather audacious promise. In all honesty, I get a little uncomfortable handling this verse because of the ways it has been misunderstood in the past. Yet it's such an important part of God's perspective on giving that we can't overlook it.

As Paul expresses it, "And God is able to make all grace abound to you, so that in all things at all times, having all that you need, you will abound in every good work" (2 Corinthians 9:8).

If that's not plain enough, he repeats it: "Now he who supplies seed to the sower and bread for food will also supply and increase your store of seed and will enlarge the harvest of your righteousness. You will be made rich in every way so that you can be generous on every occasion, and through us your generosity will result in thanksgiving to God" (2 Corinthians 9:10-11).

Paul couldn't be more explicit. When we are faithful to give generously, we do a good service to God. As a result, He will come back to us for more. When He wants to distribute again in the future, He will remember us as capable partners. If a restaurant gives good service, it results in repeat business. The same applies to good stewards. God wants to give to you so that you can give to His work. And if you sow generously, then God is able to give you more and more.

Furthermore, God takes special care of faithful stewards. As long as you are in a giving partnership with Him, He makes sure you get everything you need, exactly when you need it. That's His offer. It doesn't mean you then indulge yourself in lavish shopping sprees. That wouldn't be good stewardship. But it does mean He'll faithfully provide for your needs.

True wealth is having everything you need when you need it. And God is able to give you all things, at all times—all that you need.

Now, that should dispel all your fears about giving. In fact, there's really only one thing we should fear when it comes to giving: holding back on God to the extent that He is no longer involved in our financial lives. The question you should ask yourself is this: *Who is better able to meet my needs, me or God?* The economy won't help you. Your boss and your inheritance might not come through either. But God is able and willing to do that for you. If you're generous, He will make you rich so that you can continue to be generous. But He wants to see you investing in His kingdom first. Not in order to get what you need from Him, but because you sincerely desire to share in generous service with Him.

That's a picture of generous giving. As one writer describes this promise, "The honour of it is lasting, the reward of it eternal, and he (the giver) is still able to live comfortably himself and to give liberally to others."*

JUMPING OFF

When we started North Point Community Church, we were in a situation where we needed to raise one million dollars in four months to start our building project. So I prayed about how my wife, Sandra, and I might contribute along with everybody else. That's when I had a crazy thought. My idea was that I not take a salary from the church during the four months of fundraising. Of course, the minute I had that thought I wanted to say, "Okay God, now seriously. . . ."

* *Matthew Henry's Commentary on the Whole Bible: New Modern Edition*, Electronic Database, (Peabody, Mass.: Hendrickson, 1991).

But after talking it over with Sandra, we knew that's what we were supposed to do. Furthermore, we felt like we needed to tell our congregation, which meant we couldn't back out once we started.

After the first month of going without a salary, I got a phone call and an invitation to speak at a small men's gathering in Tennessee. I typically don't accept such engagements. But the request came from a friend and frankly, I needed some income. So, I went. After the event I expected someone to quietly hand me an envelope and thank me for participating. But no one handed me anything. I was surprised and somewhat disappointed. But that wasn't the first time something like that had happened so I didn't think much more about it. A week later I received a thank-you letter and a check for five thousand dollars. I was shocked and even a little suspicious that they might have heard about my situation and my commitment not to take a salary. So I called to find out. As it turned out, they didn't even know we were trying to raise money. It was as if God had just reached across the country and orchestrated things to channel that money in my direction. But it still wasn't four months' salary.

Then another unusual thing happened. At the end of the year, my accountant informed me that he had been going over my old tax returns and he thought the government owed me money. At first I made a joke and laughed it off. Then he told me how much money it was. As he explained it, I had been overpaying my taxes ever since I had been ordained as a minister—my entire career. And even though he could only go back four years, I ended up receiving a huge refund from the IRS that year. To make a long story short, the amount I ended up taking in from those two unlikely incidents was the equivalent of four months' salary—plus an additional seven thousand dollars!

Some people might rationalize that I just had that money coming to me anyway. It's not like it grew mysteriously on a tree in my backyard. It came in through fairly logical channels. But you know what? I'm convinced it came from God. I don't think it was just a coincidence that of all the years I had overpaid my taxes, my accountant finally noticed it that year. And I don't think it was happenstance that I got paid more than four times the amount I'd ever been paid for a speaking engagement. The way I see it, we sowed our seed for God's kingdom, and as a result God decided He could entrust even more to us. Did we take the tax money and indulge ourselves? No, we saw that money as God's too, and we stewarded it appropriately. And on and on it goes.

In reality, those types of things have happened so much in our family that when it comes to giving money, we almost expect them. Sandra and I have learned that we can't get too big a handful of seed, because God is always looking for people to resource His kingdom. And why would He shut that down?

I don't give to get rich. I'm already rich. I have two cars and a single-family house. Drop that scenario in most places around the world and I'm a very wealthy man. I give because I'm a Christian and God wants me to live like a steward. I've seen that no matter how many times I answer the call to reach into my bucket, God shows up in amazing ways.

NO FEAR

Is fear holding back your generosity? Do you give leftovers because you're concerned about making ends meet? Have you ever

asked God to give you a plan for the stewardship of His money? At some point, as a Christian, you've just got to go for it. You need to
get a big handful of seed and say, "God,
because I worry so much about money, I'm
inviting You into my finances. I want to know
that whether things are good or bad, You're
involved."

Are you ready to trade up and assume the
position God is offering you as a steward?
Are you prepared to leave fear behind and
take advantage of the law of the harvest
by inviting God to get involved in your
finances? Money is often the last door we
open to God because we think it represents
our security. But if you really want to be
secure financially, you need God involved
as soon as possible. The sooner you start
sowing seeds, the sooner you will begin
to reap a harvest. It's a principle you can
count on.

CHAPTER 4

THE NEW DEAL

❖ ❖ ❖ ❖ ❖ ❖

I've been referring to this idea of "getting God involved in your finances." Let's take a minute to explain exactly what that means. By suggesting that we can *get* God involved in our finances, I'm also suggesting that we can *keep* Him from getting involved. If we're going to walk in fields of gold some day, we need Him with us every step of the way, bringing the rain and warm sunshine that will turn dormant kernels into gilded stalks of harvestable crops.

The fact is, God can be sitting on the sidelines watching you struggle financially, or He can be actively involved as your financial partner. It all depends on what kind of steward you are. That's not to say He's like a genie who will give you what you want if you say the magic words. Nor does it mean He will never allow you to face financial hardships if you do all the "right" things. But your finances are yet another arena of life in which you can begin to experience an interactive relationship with your heavenly Father. You just need to invite Him in.

First of all, I think you already believe that God can intervene directly to change your financial picture. Here's why I think this. As a pastor, I've had plenty of chances to counsel people who were in financial trouble. And I've never heard anyone pray:

God, as You know, I've withheld from You all these years while I followed my own plan. And sure, I've gotten into this financial catastrophe while on my plan, but I still think my plan can work. So I'll figure things out here on my own, and You can go help somebody else.

No. When the bottom drops out, we suddenly want God involved in our finances. Desperately. We no longer enjoy managing our money, so we shift our strategy and start focusing on how to persuade God to come to our rescue. Have you ever reached that point?

When you do, your prayers will sound more like, *Oh, God, help! Please send some money. Please do something! Anything!*

There comes a point when you're willing to acknowledge that God controls everything. Suddenly, you're no longer bashful about asking Him to do what you've known all along He is capable of doing: to move some money here or take away some financial pressure there. In that moment, you're completely convinced of the difference He can make in your finances.

I don't need to convince you that God is sovereign over the world's wealth. I think we agree on that one.

If that's the case, then what keeps us from asking Him to get involved right now, *before* the bottom drops out? If we know deep inside that God can intervene directly in our lives like that, what are we waiting for? Doesn't it make sense to position ourselves to receive His direct intervention as soon and as often as possible? Or does that still frighten you a little?

Maybe it would help if you could know for sure when God was involved and when He wasn't. What would happen to your fear if you knew that the same God who controls the resources of the universe watches out for you, carefully channeling the perfect level of provision to meet your every need?

MORE THAN A FEELING

Let me begin with a word of caution: This isn't going to feel right. Consider this fair warning. What I'm about to tell you flies in the face of your natural instincts. It's counterintuitive, directly opposite of what you think you should do. If you're going to get God involved in your finances, you need to understand that there will be moments when it's not 100 percent comfortable. Or even 50 percent. You're going to have to be willing to trust something besides your gut because your gut is simply not a good gauge.

Remember, fear and uncertainty make us irrational. And if we respond out of fear, we often end up doing very irrational, destructive things financially. Moreover, since money is an emotional subject, we're especially vulnerable to irrational thinking when it comes to our finances. That's why it's so important to base your financial decisions on truth rather than instinct. You would never advise someone to buy a stock just because it felt right. You would first examine things like price/earnings ratios and earnings per share.

Likewise, you should be careful not to allow your financial theology to be corrupted by emotion. If we decide to hold back from God because it "doesn't feel right," our giving is based on emotion rather than truth. This sort of irrational thinking will keep you from enlisting the God of the universe to be involved in your finances. Isn't that like being afraid to call the police to save you from an armed robber because police carry guns too? Or avoiding the doctor because you're afraid he might give you a shot, a shot that could save your life? And yet when we withhold from God financially, we distance ourselves from the one person in the universe who can forever dispel our fears about making ends meet. It's like saying, "I'm going to protect myself financially by withholding from God and making sure He's not involved in my finances."

That, my friend, is completely irrational.

PACK UP YOUR TROUBLES

If you could take each of your financial concerns and personally ask God about them, wouldn't you like to know what He would say?

"But God, what if we can't buy groceries?"

"But God, shouldn't we save for a rainy day?"

"But God, what if one of us gets sick?"

All those concerns are valid. And it's a little hard to be generous when you're overwhelmed with concerns. But God has a strategy for handling your concerns, a strategy that, in turn, frees you up to trust Him with your resources.

Jesus spoke directly to this point. In fact, He described the relationship between your physical needs and your fears. During His keynote address, the Sermon on the Mount, Jesus said:

> *"Therefore I tell you, do not worry about your life, what you will eat or drink; or about your body, what you will wear. . . . So do not worry, saying, 'What shall we eat?' or 'What shall we drink?' or 'What shall we wear?' For the pagans run after all these things, and your heavenly Father knows that you need them. But seek first his kingdom and his righteousness, and all these things will be given to you as well."*
>
> (MATTHEW 6:25, 31-33)

"What will we eat?" "What will we drink?" "What will we wear?" Sound familiar? Most of our budget concerns fall into one of those categories. And yet Jesus says not to worry about them at all. Instead, we should focus on something else entirely: His kingdom. And when we do, He says our physical needs will be met as well.

You've probably heard this passage all your life. But have you ever really thought about what it says? What if you got up tomorrow and instead of thinking about how to make a living, you thought about giving? "Hey, I'm going to work today, and I can't wait until payday because I really need to make another gift to my church." Or "Honey, we've really outgrown this worship center, so I'm thinking about taking a second job so we can build a larger building and have enough room for everybody... oh, and by the way, we had a little money left over this month so why don't we go to the grocery store for some food?"

We don't think like that, do we? We get up and go to work primarily so we can eat. And once our basic needs are met, we think about giving. But Jesus says, "Hey, from now on, it's the other way around." In essence, He took

Maslow's hierarchy of needs and flipped it upside down. It's enough to make anyone tremble with uncertainty. Doesn't something inside you want to say, *Where is the relationship between giving to God's kingdom and being able to buy groceries? It doesn't make sense.* It certainly doesn't appeal to conventional wisdom. So unless you look outside normal logic, you won't be able to embrace this promise as it was meant to be embraced. And you may never confront your fears about claiming it in your own life.

There, at the center of Jesus' teaching, is a new deal for anyone who will follow Him. The deal is simple. When you make God's kingdom your first priority, He promises to provide what you need to live. In other words Jesus is saying, "If you will be about *My* needs—taking care of the poor and making disciples—I will be about *your* needs." And just like you and me, Jesus' audiences lived in a world devoid of physical and financial certainty. Nevertheless, He promised that if they kept their end of the deal, He would—with certainty—meet their needs. And He can only make that promise if indeed He is in control of the world's economy. Including yours and mine.

The fact that God would invite me into a symbiotic relationship with Him is an amazing thought to me. Imagine a holy, all-powerful God devising a mutually beneficial arrangement with me, demoting His plans to such a level that I am able to play a part in bringing them to fruition. As if He really needs me. God can do whatever He wants with or without my financial help. He doesn't need my money. It's all His anyway. Nevertheless, because He loves us so much and longs to interact with us, He invites us into a trade relationship in which we contribute to His needs and He contributes to ours. So that's how this new deal works. When you partner with God to fulfill His plan for the world, He takes a vested interest in your well-being. He wants you eating well and living indoors so you can continue to resource His kingdom.

Now you have a choice to make. If you want God involved in your finances, you need to put your finances to work for God's interests. And that means you need to give. You can start right now with what He's already given you. That might mean a percentage of your next paycheck. It might mean a part of your net worth. Wherever the voice of generosity leads you, you need to follow it, in spite of the fear you may feel.

Your financial fears aren't going away until you act. You can face them alone, using your best instincts and wisdom. Or you can embrace, once and for all, the counterintuitive logic of the God who controls everything. Do you want God involved in your finances? Do you want His guarantee that you'll have something to eat and drink, and clothes to wear? Then you need to focus on His agenda. And financially, that means answering the call to sow generously into His kingdom.

If you don't want Him involved, or if you aren't sure, that's fine. But let me make a prediction. There will come a day when you realize your need for Him. When the financial going gets tough enough, and your fear of trusting yourself finally exceeds your fear of trusting God, you will call for His help. It's only a matter of time.

Jesus' words are difficult. They're a stumbling block for human logic. How can giving result in my needs being met? How can subtracting from my monthly cash flow add to it? How can stepping toward financial uncertainty lead to the greatest financial security available in the world? You'll never know until you try it.

A GAME OF OPPOSITES

You'd think we'd all have a pretty good handle on fear. Everyone knows that emotions are never very trustworthy guides. You can sit in a safe, climate-controlled movie theater with hot popcorn and a cold drink, and yet your emotions can be in complete upheaval because of what's being projected on the screen. Statistically, your greatest risk of injury from a commercial plane trip is in the car driving to the airport, but guess which part makes people's palms sweat. Our emotions rarely follow reality. Much of the time they actually tell us the reverse of what's true. It's like they're playing a game of opposites.

In the mountains of North Georgia is Camp Highland, a camp that uses high adventure elements as object lessons for life. The highlight of the camp is the high-ropes course. Talk about fear. Just the thought of leaping from the top of a telephone pole to a trapeze seven feet away is enough to make my heart race. Another element of the course is called "the Drop Zone." The name alone elicits fear. But I love what the high ropes course illustrates about trusting emotions versus trusting God. Once you're secured to the safety system with an OSHA-approved harness, your fears are no longer justified. In fact, they're irrational. But knowing this doesn't make them go away. The high ropes course is a perfect picture of how we let perception and misperception influence our decisions and our course in life—especially in the area of finances. Even when we're securely in the grip of God's safety harness, it's so difficult to take that first step toward generosity.

In case you ever go to a place like Camp Highland and get the chance to walk a tightrope forty feet off the ground or make a freefall from a platform at the top of a tree, I'll let you in on a little secret only the insiders know. If you want to have fun instead of being terrified all day, there's a simple step you can take that instantly disarms the whole fear of falling.

As soon as you put on your safety harness, hook it up to the safety cable overhead and hang from it. Just sit down in your harness. Before you take a single step out on the ropes or leave the safety of Earth, let yourself feel what would happen if you did fall. It's amazing. Once people realize that—thanks to the safety system—falling is no big deal, they typically face the ropes elements with a level of confidence they hadn't possessed before.

The same is true of generous giving. When you let yourself feel what would happen if you trusted God to provide for your needs, it instantly changes your perspective forever.

If God were involved in your finances, would you feel more secure or less? And if you can trust God to bail you out of a financial emergency, doesn't it make sense that He could keep you from getting into one in the first place?

So what's more rational?

Clearly, God won't force His way into our wallets. He waits for us to invite Him to be the Lord of our possessions and to get involved in our finances. And that means giving from what you've already got, whether it's tithing on your income, giving from your net worth, or contributing whatever amount He puts on your heart. Sure, that means giving up some control. It means inviting Him to give you a financial mission that's bigger than you are. That can be overwhelming, but wouldn't it be sad to miss out on such an opportunity?

Again, this isn't about giving to get. It's not about getting on God's meal ticket. It's about neutralizing the fears that have been hindering the spirit of generosity inside you. It's about discovering the thrill of taking part in God's plan for the universe and experiencing the security that comes from knowing that your provider is the One who owns all provisions. When we sow, God shows up in amazing ways. And once you experience the perfect provision of a loving heavenly Father, all fear will begin to evaporate.

CHAPTER 5

SOWING LESSONS

After reading the last four chapters, you might be ready to invite God into the realm of your finances. You're ready to face your fears and start sowing. You've decided that you can't expect a crop without scattering your seed. You can picture the rolling fields of gold that are shimmering under the gentle wind of the Spirit, and now you're ready to begin sowing in faith.

Maybe you're wondering, *How much do I give? Where do I give it? When do I give?* Let's look at some very practical steps to follow for sowing.

GOD'S PLAN FOR GIVING

There's a simple principle in Scripture that provides an answer to the question of "How much?" The idea comes from the same passage we looked at earlier in 2 Corinthians. In these verses, the apostle Paul explains exactly how much you should give:

Each man should give what he has decided in his heart to give, not reluctantly or under compulsion, for God loves a cheerful giver.
(2 CORINTHIANS 9:7)

Perhaps you were expecting something that looks a little more like a financial plan. Paul doesn't offer any calculations of gross and net, nor does he share depreciation schedules or dividend tables. He just says to give whatever you decide in your heart to give. That's it. And while it may not seem like a very substantive answer, it's the only answer we need to guide our giving.

In a way, the plan is refreshingly simple. He doesn't name a percentage or particular amount. And there's no hint of pressure. He says, "Not reluctantly or under compulsion, for God loves a cheerful giver."

In this statement, Paul eliminates the idea of giving reactively or out of guilt. In other words, if that's how you feel about giving, God says, "That's okay, you just keep it. I'll use somebody else's." God knows that someone who gives reluctantly is still thinking like an owner, not a steward. And rather than take your money and allow you to miss the whole point, God says, "No, you don't understand. I want us to be partners, with Me as the owner and you as the steward."

When you begin to embrace your role as a steward, you will be able to give from your heart. You'll see yourself in partnership with God to accomplish eternal purposes and you will even start to think about creating a plan for giving. A steward doesn't wait until the offering plate is passed to decide how much to give. It's something to which he gives a great deal of thought because it's something that means a lot to him. He understands why he's giving and can visualize the impact his gift will have on the recipient. It's very motivating when you approach giving like a steward.

In contrast, when you give under compulsion, you don't put much thought into it. This kind of giving is usually an impulsive response to a request. It can be accompanied by guilt, pressure, or a fear of embarrassment. And it's typically a gift given from leftovers.

We've already seen that God loves a cheerful giver. He doesn't want you to give reactively. He wants you to go home, look at your bucket of seed, and determine in your heart how much you'd like to sow. He wants you to consider thoughtfully your current circumstances, your life, your potential, and your finances. He wants you to involve your family. He wants you to pray about it. And then He wants you to come up with a plan. It may be a percentage or an amount. But the idea is that you sit down when your mind is clear and you say, "God, here's the bucket You've blessed me with. Now I want You to help me determine a percentage or an amount of seed, and then I'm going to make up my mind."

Then, whether times are good or bad, you stick faithfully to the plan God gives you. As you do, God will return to you and bless you according to what you have given. It's not a promise to get rich. It's a promise that the God of all earthly treasures wants to involve you in distributing His wealth to fund His worldwide purposes.

Giving should be a relational experience. If you don't feel closer to God—as if He's compelling you to give and your gifts are an expression of your heartfelt devotion back to Him—then you may be missing the whole point of giving. Giving involves mathematics, so there's always the potential for it to become a lifeless formula or a legalistic duty. But that's not how biblical, New Testament giving should work. If your policy is to give as you have decided in your heart, you'll find that giving won't be something that's robotic, passionless, or routine.

THE PLAN TAKES SHAPE

It's clear that cheerful generosity is to be the backbone of your giving plan. But let's face it: relying on waves of generosity isn't much of a plan by itself. So let's go a step further and give some practical structure to your generosity. These helpful guidelines will keep you pointed in the right direction.

I'd like to present a plan that will help quantify all this advice about giving. Of course, this isn't a black-and-white, step-by-step sort of thing. But it is a blueprint that will keep you in sync with God's heart on giving. For starters, the simple idea of having a plan is a biblical concept, not to mention a good idea (see Deuteronomy 14:22). I don't think it's enough to only give "as the Spirit leads," that is, whenever the idea hits you. Sure, God will lead you to give spontaneously from time to time, and generosity should always be your overriding motive. But the idea of planning is central to what the Bible says about finances. Besides, giving without a plan leaves you vulnerable to your own emotions, and as we've seen, emotions can be influenced by fear. So the best strategy for giving is a twofold approach: a basic plan combined with a willingness to consider spontaneous giving when unique opportunities arise.

PART ONE: THE THREE P'S
Let's start with a basic plan. A good plan will provide guidelines to help you navigate through the practical issues of giving, such as how much to give and when to give. If you examine everything the Bible has to say about giving, several recurring themes emerge. While it doesn't tell you exactly what to do in every situation, the Bible does identify key principles to help you make good decisions and develop a solid plan for your giving. Just as a good educational plan builds on the "three R's," a good plan for giving builds on the "three P's"—Priority giving, Percentage giving, and Progressive giving.

PRIORITY GIVING

The first P stands for *priority*. Of all the items in your monthly budget, giving should be the top priority. Not just *a* priority, but the first one. In other words, before you pay the mortgage or buy groceries or pay the other bills, the very first check you need to write is to your local church and other ministries you support. Here's why: If you wait until other expenses are met first, it will impact the bottom line of your giving. That's just the way it works with priorities. Whatever you place first will take precedence over everything that comes after it. As we just discussed, generosity should play a key role in guiding your giving. In fact, God means for it to be the primary impetus behind your giving plan. And your generosity tends to be highest immediately after receiving provision. Waiting until that provision has dwindled and been reduced by your monthly obligations has a tendency to squelch generosity. However, if you prioritize your giving, then everything else will take its proper place in line behind the priority of God's work.

By prioritizing God in your checkbook ledger, you avoid running short when it comes time to give Him His share. Imagine having

God over to a big dinner party, but serving His plate last. Oops! The food runs out right before it gets to Him, so you go to the refrigerator and scrape together some leftovers. You would never do that to God. And you shouldn't do it with your finances either. Set aside His portion first, and you won't dishonor your most important guest.

My wife is a wonderful cook. And whenever we have company for dinner, a strange sequence of events unfolds. No matter how much food we have on hand, Sandra makes a special trip to the grocery store to buy the ingredients for the menu she plans to serve our guests. It's not that we don't already have food in our house. But part of hosting friends is preparing a meal especially for them. Then, after the guests have enjoyed the meal, our family gets to enjoy the leftovers from that meal the next day. Granted, we could probably find plenty of leftovers in our refrigerator to feed our guests, but it's more appropriate to honor company with the first servings and give ourselves the leftovers.

When it comes to giving to God, things should work the same way. We should honor God with the first portion of our income instead of giving Him the leftovers. That means when you get your paycheck, write a check for God's portion first. Then, use the leftovers to meet your own needs like paying bills or buying groceries. That's the definition of priority giving.

PERCENTAGE GIVING

The second P stands for *percentage*. What I like most about the idea of percentage giving is that it objectifies the whole giving process. Remember, the more you can do to keep fear from influencing your wallet, the less you risk drifting away from God in your finances. When you commit to give a percentage of your income, it's pretty cut and dry. The numbers don't lie. Ten percent is still 10 percent, whether you feel confident that your heavenly Father will provide your needs or not. So whatever percentage you choose, you have a target you can aim for no matter how much your emotions fluctuate.

Now let me shed some light on tithing—giving 10 percent of your income. I could present all kinds of scholarly dissections of the Old Testament, then reconcile Levitical Law against the New Testament's theology of grace. But that's not really necessary.

Picture yourself receiving ten one-dollar bills from God. Remember, God is the owner and you're just a steward, not an owner. As you look at the bills in your hand, you say, "God, You're handing me ten of Your dollars. What do You want me to do with them? Are You going to want them back?"

God says, "I just want one of them back."

Puzzled, you reply, "Just one? Are you sure?"

"Yep. Just give me one," He says.

"Well, what do You want me to do with the other nine?" you inquire.

"Whatever you want," He replies.

"You mean You're giving me ten dollars, and You want only one back —and I get to keep the other nine for me?" you exclaim in disbelief.

You get the idea. Can you imagine hiring a money manager to steward your 401(k) and telling him he can keep 90 percent of it? That's basically what God does with you. If you think about it, all God asks for His investment is a tenth of the principal. It's almost laughable. And to think we struggle to give Him any of it.

If you truly approach your finances as if God were the owner of it all, giving a percentage back to Him is only appropriate. And if

you're searching the Bible for a percentage
that you can be sure is pleasing to Him—
whether you want to call it obedience or just
cheerful giving—10 percent is a good place
to start (see Genesis 28:22). It was the amount
observed in the Old Testament, so there's
something about that amount that God has
decided is appropriate. Maybe He knows
some elaborate formula and 10 percent is the
precise amount that will keep our hearts from
drifting as our wealth fluctuates. I'm not sure
why. But when God spoke on the subject, He
required 10 percent. And while the Old Testament days are long gone, 10 percent is still
a good reference point for our giving today.

So are you willing to try 10 percent? Or is
that still a little too scary?

Whether you're ready to tithe or not, I
want to encourage you to pick a number
and begin percentage giving. It's the best
way to create benchmarks and get a handle
on an otherwise intangible decision-making
process. What percentage can you see yourself giving? How about 5 percent? Even if
your knees are quivering and you can only
muster 1 percent, I urge you to commit to
something and stick to it. If you need more
discipline, establish a time frame to work

within. Try it for thirty or sixty days and watch what happens.

It's so important to start somewhere, anywhere. Because until you try it, you won't put yourself in a position to experience the intervention of the Creator of all economy as He begins to move in the area of your finances. And once you encounter Him firsthand, your motivation will skyrocket. So pick your percentage and start with your next paycheck.

Finally, a lot of people ask me about tithing on gross income versus tithing on the net. To that I reply with a question: "What kind of harvest do you want, net or gross?" Remember, you're sowing. And you will reap what you sow. You will be rewarded in eternity for the way you handle your finances today. Do you want a gross reward or a net reward? For me, tithing on the gross amount is a reasonable proposition. I've found that you can adjust your lifestyle to fit just about any variable once you make up your mind to do so.

PROGRESSIVE GIVING

The third P stands for *progressive*, and that means progressively increasing the percentage you give over the years. If you've been giving 10 percent for several years, maybe it's time to move up to 12 percent or 15. Here's why I think this is a good idea. Your faith and your faithfulness grow hand in hand. You can't separate them. And if your faith is to thrive and grow, your faithfulness must also develop.

As long as you are alive on this earth, God intends for your faith to be growing. His agenda for your life is that you be gradually transformed, little by little, to the likeness of Christ. That's the nature of faith. Its progress is steady, and its target is Christ-likeness.

Now, when it comes to your finances, you need to be growing in faith there as well. But you can't grow as a giver if you don't also increase your giving. In other words, if you've been tithing for twenty years and you've never increased your percentage of giving, you haven't grown. Sure, you've been faithful in terms of steadfastness. And that's great. But in order for your faith to grow, it needs to be stretched from time to time. And that means progressively increasing the percentage you entrust to God as the owner of your finances.

Over the years, Sandra and I have been challenged to bump up our giving on several occasions. It's not every year, but we can usually tell when it's time to rethink our goals. When you first start tithing, it's such a spiritual experience. You can hardly believe you're voluntarily doing something with your money that flies in the face of normal economics. But the thrill of honoring God while also trusting Him to intervene on your behalf makes it irresistible. It's exciting because you encounter God through it all.

After a while, it's easy to tithe. It becomes second nature, like a reflex you hardly notice anymore. But giving should always be an exciting, spiritual, close-encounter-with-God experience. So if it has become a mundane routine, then maybe it's time to stretch your financial faith a little. As you give to fund God's needs, are you forced to trust Him to provide for yours?

That's what a growing faith is all about. And over the long haul, it's not enough just to commit to a percentage. Growth means reviewing your giving goals and occasionally increasing the percentage you give.

PART TWO: PROMPTED GIVING (THE FOURTH P)

Now let's talk about the second part of our twofold strategy for giving: the willingness to consider spontaneous giving for unique opportunities that arise. You can think of this part as the fourth P: *Prompted Giving.*

Having a plan is important. But from time to time, God may prompt you to make a special gift that goes beyond a rote formula. It can be the most relational experience in all your giving. There's nothing like knowing that God is living and moving and interacting with you. In this way, God uses promptings to communicate that you are in a unique position to meet His kingdom needs.

I spoke once at a youth camp in Alabama. The music leader for the camp was a delightful fellow with a heart for God and he had traveled a long way to lead worship for the camp. During that week, Sandra and I learned that the music leader and his wife were expecting their first child. They were very excited, but the medical costs of delivering a baby were really stretching them financially.

About halfway through the week, God prompted me: *Why not give this fellow your honorarium for speaking at the camp?* Sandra and I talked it over and agreed to do it. It was a little scary because we didn't even know how much I would receive. What if it was a large amount, more than we meant to give the fellow? But we decided to give the couple whatever we received for speaking at the camp. And we did.

That's what I mean by prompted giving. It wasn't part of our regular tithe. It was over and above. And as we learned in a letter we received several weeks later, God used that gift in a powerful way to help that couple meet the expenses of having a baby.

Prompted giving changes your perspective. You no longer view God as a vending machine. Instead, you begin to see Him as your personal heavenly Father. As you walk through life, He constantly introduces you to people with needs. Sometimes it's a spiritual need; other times it's a physical need. Sometimes you're the one in need, and other times you provide what's needed. This is how the church body works. In fact, it's how the human race works. As stewards, we have the privilege of interacting with our heavenly Father and ministering to the needs of His children in the world. Without the element of promptings in your giving, the whole process could become very cold and calculated. Promptings are the pulse in the church body.

In 1 John 3:17, Jesus asks, "If anyone has material possessions and sees his brother in need but has no pity on him, how can the love of God be in him?" God uses the needs of others as opportunities for us to exhibit His love alive in us. And many times those opportunities are revealed through special promptings that are above and beyond your regular, scheduled giving.

I give our three children a regular allowance. But every once in a while I give them extra spending money for something special, like a vacation. It's not an either/or proposition. I give them both. Giving to God's kingdom is the same way. If you see your brother in need, it doesn't matter if you already gave somewhere else. You should be open to the idea of God using you to meet your brother's unexpected need.

THE GOD FACTOR

There you have it, a comprehensive outline for giving. It includes a basic plan built around the three P's, and it is sensitive to promptings from God to meet special kingdom needs that may arise.

Now let's talk a little more about fear. You may be looking at this plan on paper with your own salary and expenses plugged into the columns and you're thinking, *We can't afford to do that!* If that's your reaction, there's one part of the equation you've forgotten to include: the God factor.

As a pastor, I have a front row seat to some of the most incredible financial stories you've ever heard. Over the years, I've talked to hundreds of people who were in debt or had a negative cash flow, and it just made no sense for them to give money away to a church or a ministry. But somehow, once they scraped up the courage to give it a shot, their lives began to change. Time after time, I've heard stories of people on the other side of that initial fear of tithing. And consistently they report back that once they started giving, God got involved in their finances. Money arrived unexpectedly. Debt was repaid in a fraction of the time they had projected. I'm not trying to sound mystical. But those people are living proof that giving can open the door to your heavenly Father's involvement in your finances.

One such couple, Rudy and Trina, had nearly twenty thousand dollars in credit card debt, a mortgage, two car payments, and a student loan. They were barely getting by.

To top it off, they had just learned that Trina was pregnant and that her job would be phased out by the time she returned to work from maternity leave. They didn't know what to do. That Sunday, I was speaking on the idea of tithing and getting God involved in your finances. After the sermon, Rudy and Trina approached me with some questions. "Are you saying we should start giving now, while things are more upside down than ever?" they asked. I assured them I thought that even someone in their position should get involved in stewarding possessions right away.

Almost two years later, I got a letter from Rudy and Trina. Their little boy had just started walking. They were writing to tell me that although it didn't make sense at the time, they had decided to follow my advice about giving. "Andy, I can't begin to describe how good it feels to be debt free!" they shared. They went on to explain that within a few weeks of their experiment in tithing, several earthshaking events took place that impacted their finances. First, the large company where Trina was employed became involved in a lawsuit over the issue of maternity leave. While the case had nothing to do with Trina, the company took immediate measures to protect itself from further trouble by enacting sweeping new employment policies. As a result, Trina was given a special compensation package that put an unexpected $35,000 in her pocket—enough to pay off the credit card debt and the student loan. In addition, Trina was offered the chance to create a new position for herself in which she would be allowed to work from home.

Meanwhile, Rudy experienced a windfall of his own. Unexpectedly, three of the vice presidents over him were hired away by other companies. In the shuffle, Rudy was promoted to a position that normally would have taken several years to achieve. Between his new company car and the promotion bonus, Rudy was able to eliminate their two car loans as well. His new salary was so generous, they even decided that Trina could afford to quit her job completely and focus on being a full-time mom.

But the best thing about Rudy and Trina's letter was their exuberance over the mission works they had helped to fund. They shared several stories about opportunities they had had to become involved in evangelism projects and to give spontaneously to meet the needs of several families in their town. They truly understood their role as stewards of God's resources.

The amazing thing about Rudy and Trina's story is how often I hear others just like it. It doesn't make sense on paper, but then there's the God factor. In so many cases, God is just waiting to get involved in the finances of His children. We just need to trust Him enough to take the first step and sow our seed.

And when you experience your heavenly Father's love as He meets your needs, your fear will have met its match. Because perfect love casts out fear.

CHAPTER 6

FEAR THIS

✤ ✤ ✤ ✤ ✤ ✤

The human race is notorious for being afraid
of the wrong things. The trail of history is
littered with discarded fears that once erro-
neously controlled mankind's destiny. In
hindsight, it's easy to see their absurdity.

Many of man's ancient fears have been
upended in a complete reversal of thinking.
Where man once feared evil spirits as the
cause of headaches, he soon developed a
greater fear of having a hole bored in his skull
to let them out. The fear of witches in Salem,
Massachusetts, was gradually replaced by the
fear of a judicial system that was starting to
behave like a bunch of lunatics. For centuries,
the fear of falling off the earth kept Europeans

from discovering America, until finally, the fear of missing out on vast new resources replaced it. As children, we fear the first day of school. But wisdom prevails when we begin to fear growing up without an education. The fear of going to the dentist must be weighed against the fear of losing your teeth to neglect. The list goes on and on.

All fears are assigned a certain pecking order, with some fears ranking higher than others. The fact is, fear replaces fear. One way to fight fear is to supplant it with other fears that outrank it. One thing is clear. Fear is here to stay; it's at the heart of our frail humanity. We spend much of our lives avoiding fear. But for all our efforts, it never goes away. Not a single generation has managed to exist fear-free. For most of us, not a day goes by without some element of fear.

So we must conclude that fear is not so much something to be avoided as it is something to be leveraged. If fear were water, the idea would not be to stay dry, because that's futile. The idea is to catch a wave and ride fear to a golden shore. You see, fear can actually be a good thing. The fear of danger is beneficial when it acts to preserve life. The fear of failure is productive when it spurs us toward success. And Proverbs teaches that the fear of the Lord is the beginning of wisdom (Proverbs 9:10). So the idea is not to avoid fear, but to choose our fears wisely. We become irrational when we fear the wrong things. Prioritizing our fears improperly can actually put us in greater jeopardy.

The sooner you spread your fears out on the table and prioritize them, the better. Analyze your fears for their true potency, then prioritize them accordingly. Which fears really warrant your attention? And which ones are ultimately benign? Wisdom is the key to sorting through your fears.

However, the more threatening the fears, the more difficult it is to apply wisdom and sort them out. Which ranks higher, the fear of reporting physical abuse or the fear of keeping quiet? Abuse victims struggle to know. It's the same on a global level. Is it more fearful to confront the tyranny of a Hitler, a Castro, or a Saddam Hussein, or is it even more terrifying to ignore it? When life and death hang on our decisions, wisdom seems elusive.

COMPOUNDED TROUBLE

When it comes to your money, what should you fear most? Which fears should take priority? Which sets of concerns should drive your financial decisions? If you're like me, you worry at times about your ability to survive a major economic down-turn. Perhaps you fear some sort of personal tragedy that could sink you financially. Then, there's always the "What if I get sick?" nightmare.

There are good reasons for us to be careful about how we invest our money. Those are the fears that generally drive us to stockpile our money so that we will be able to navigate successfully through the "what-ifs" that haunt us. But as we have seen, those same fears also have the potential to weaken our resolve to give.

On the other side of the fear continuum are the insights we have just discussed. Instead of fearing the prospects of facing financial challenges without enough savings, we ought to fear facing the same scenario without our heavenly Father standing on the front lines with us. Think about it: What do you fear most? Not having enough, or not having the involvement of your heavenly Father? Your answer to that question will determine what you do for the future.

Ironically enough, as I write this chapter,

I am looking back on two very disappointing years in regard to my personal wealth. Like many Americans, I watched my carefully invested portfolio dwindle to half of its value. As I look back, do you know what I regret most? I don't wish I had kept everything in cash. I wish I had given more of it away. At least then I would have something to show for it. As it stands now, I'm less financially secure and less invested in kingdom work than I was before.

Jesus told a story in Matthew 25 that illustrates this point perfectly. In the parable, there was a steward who was given something to invest. But instead of investing it, he buried it to keep it safe. Explaining his behavior later, he shared that he had been afraid of investing it poorly and losing it: "Master, . . . I knew that you are a hard man, . . . so I was afraid and went out and hid your talent in the ground" (Matthew 25:24-25). The steward thought it would be better to play it safe and at least return the property in full when the owner returned. So he acted on his fear by disobeying the owner's instructions. He thought wrong.

Suddenly a new fear gripped the steward's heart as he realized the full consequences of his actions. The new fear was of something far worse than the one he had entertained in the beginning when he decided to bury the talent. "Throw that worthless servant outside, into the darkness," the master ranted to his guards, "where there will be weeping and gnashing of teeth" (Matthew 25:30).

As it turned out, this steward failed to assess his fears, prioritizing his fears incorrectly; while he was afraid on the front end, his lack of wisdom caused even greater fear on the back end. He didn't solve his fear problem by acting on it. In fact, by doing nothing, he actually compounded his fear.

So, let me ask you one more time: What do you fear most? Not having enough or not having the involvement of your heavenly Father in the realm of your finances? If the uncertainty of the future is your greatest concern, you will seek first your own kingdom. If your fear of not having enough is trumped by your fear of missing out on God's involvement in your finances, you will seek His kingdom first. You will sow generously, fearlessly, intentionally. And the result will be a peace that defies human logic, a joy that makes mere happiness pale in comparison.

What you fear most will determine

whether you merely save for the future or give for the future.

WHEN TIME EXPIRES

The book and Academy Award-winning movie *Schindler's List* chronicles the true story of one man's effort to make the most of a desperate opportunity. As the director of a munitions factory in Nazi Germany, Oskar Schindler decides to leverage his position to save the lives of Jews. By employing them in his factory, Schindler is able to pluck condemned Jews from the gas chambers. But keeping them on is costly. Little by little, he liquidates his personal possessions in order to keep the business productive and underwrite the lives of his employees. Carefully, he budgets his resources to help as many people as possible without going under financially.

At the end of the story, the Nazis are defeated. The full weight of Schindler's efforts is finally revealed as the dead are counted and the living stagger back to freedom. In the midst of this denouement, Oskar Schindler has a startling realization: He could have saved even more. Overwhelmed with horrifying regret, he laments the few goods still remaining in his possession, goods that could have been liquidated to save Jews from death. If only he had known when the war would end, he could have done more. But now it is too late.

Oskar Schindler was a hero. He is credited with saving more lives during World War II than any other single person. But interestingly enough, all he could think about was what he didn't do. He wished he had done more.

We can learn a powerful lesson about giving from this example. Because in the same way, even generous Christians will probably look back on their lives and wish they had given more. And for those who never sowed at all, imagine the horror of their regret when they have to give an account for their finances in this lifetime.

If we allow our fear of poverty to control us now, we'll have even more to fear in the end when we lose everything. But if we apply wisdom and start now to avert the inevitable fear and regret, we'll have nothing to fear in the end.

ECONOMICS 101

A good friend of mine, Mike Kendrick, runs an investment banking company that provides financial capital for growing companies. During the heyday of the Internet, his company employed a staff of dozens and required a large office in North Atlanta.

Mike takes his role as a steward very seriously. So when times were good, he spent a lot of time thinking of ways to leverage his possessions for God's kingdom. In addition to giving financially, Mike had a breakthrough idea: Why not use his platform as a business owner to help fledgling ministries get off the ground? At first, he invited several ministries to use his extra office space, saving them thousands each month in overhead. But he didn't stop there. Using his mind for business, Mike packaged the idea into a formal business model and started exporting it, convincing other Christian business owners to do the same with their extra resources. Some gave office space, while others donated valuable services such as accounting, legal, and administrative help.

Before long, dozens of ministries were applying to Ministry Ventures for help in bringing their vision of serving God to reality. Many of those ministries owe their existence to Mike and his dream of leveraging his resources for God's kingdom.

Then something unexpected happened, forcing Mike to rework his business model in order to survive. But in the midst of what turned out to be a financial nightmare, Mike experienced God's provision and protection. Throughout the entire ordeal, he sensed God's presence. In his heart he knew that ultimately things would work out. After all, through his generosity and good steward-ship, he had invited the Creator of economy to be his business partner. He had nothing to fear.

Mike landed on his feet financially and spiritually. Although his net worth was sig-nificantly reduced, his faith was stronger than ever. And as he sifted through the remains of his financial world, he discovered that some of his investments continued to pay big dividends in spite of the economy—the investments he had made in kingdom work.

As he looked around, dozens of new min-istries were thriving, thanks to his generosity during the good times. In essence, the things Mike could have kept for himself would have been reduced to half, or less, of their value. But everything he had given away flourished. Like the farmer who sows generously, Mike found himself surrounded by fields of healthy, golden wheat, a harvest that survived the economic drought.

In many ways, Mike was the embodiment of Jesus' words when he said, "The man who loves his life will lose it, while the man who hates his life in this world will keep it for eternal life" (John 12:25). By looking beyond the temporary to the eternal, Mike found the courage to sow toward what lasts forever. In doing so, he discovered a profound truth: What is given away cannot be taken away. Money invested in God's kingdom is immediately out of reach of the most turbulent of economic conditions. It is the most secure of all investments.

Financial uncertainty is a reality. As much as we work to insulate ourselves from every eventuality, the truth is, none of us is completely immune to economic upheaval, whether it's personal or corporate. When the unexpected rolls around, we will be affected. Our net worth, and possibly our income, will be impacted. And in those times when everything seems to be up for grabs, we will long for the assurance that we are not alone. We will want to know with certainty that as we cast our financial cares upon our heavenly Father, He will, in fact, care for us (see 1 Peter 5:7).

Your certainty then hinges on your generosity now. Your willingness to invest in the Father's kingdom now will be reflected in His involvement in your finances both now and then. This is why it is imperative that you sow generously when you can. But as Mike Kendrick's adventure illustrates so well, that is only half the story.

Beyond the personal peace that comes with knowing that we do not face turbulent times alone, there is the joy that comes with knowing that a portion of our wealth can't be touched by the economic turbulence of this world. All that has been invested outside of our personal kingdoms will bear fruit for eternity.

I have another friend named David Wills who works with an organization that teaches people how to become generous givers. David told me about a conversation he had with an eighty-three-year-old gentleman who had a net worth of thirty million dollars. David was trying to help this man overcome his fear of giving. But the gentleman just couldn't let go of his hard-earned money. David did his best to help the fellow see that parting with up to one-third of his money would still leave him in great shape financially. At that point, the man turned to David and said, "Young man, you have a thing or two to learn about economics. I lived during the Great Depression. I was a wealthy man then. I watched well over thirty million dollars of personal wealth evaporate almost overnight."

He was afraid. And with good reason. For a moment David was speechless. His first inclination was to encourage the man to keep working and saving. And he confided to me later that the man's story made him feel a little fearful about his own situation. After all, if a guy with thirty million dollars isn't safe, who is?

But then David asked him to ponder this thought. "Imagine how you would feel today if you had given half your wealth away just before the economic disaster in 1929." The man thought for a moment and smiled. He then wrote David a large check for a list of kingdom-oriented non-profit organizations. That day he gave away about 8 percent of his wealth. Two years later he died and gave the rest away as well.

Right now, as you read these words, you

have a wonderful opportunity. With the flick of a pen, you can invite your heavenly Father into the world of your finances, while at the same time insuring that a portion of your wealth is untouchable by both personal and national tragedies.

What's there to fear?

CHAPTER 7

THE JOY
OF GIVING

If you're like me, right about now you're wondering how well you really reflect this idea of fearless giving. When someone presents a standard, we want to know how we measure up. So I want to leave you with a clear view of the bull's-eye on the target of fearless giving.

We've already talked about percentages and other helpful ways to measure your progress on this journey. But I don't want those things to distract you from the whole point of fearless giving. You see, the four P's are great guidelines to follow. But the ultimate reward of moving beyond fear in this area is not something you measure in financial terms at all. The crowning achievement of overcoming the fear of giving is the moment you begin to experience the joy of giving. If I could give you a target to shoot for, that would be it. Like I suggested at the start, it's not so much about percentages or dollar amounts. It's more about a condition of the heart. And the opposite of a fearful heart is not a courageous heart, as you might expect. It's a joyful heart.

There's no better way to measure it. You'll know you've gotten beyond your fear when you begin to experience joy in the act of giving. It may not happen instantly. It may come so gradually that you hardly notice it. But little by little, you'll know you've arrived when the thrill of making a financial impact begins to consume you and fill you with joy.

All around the world, churches are filled with people who are motivated to give to fulfill the commands of Scripture. That's a start. The goal is to discover the joy of living in an intimate financial partnership with our heavenly Father. And when we do, giving becomes an exciting, passion-filled act of worship. But at some point, giving must move from the "have to" column to the "want to" column of our lives. That

won't happen until we wrestle our fears
to the ground.

So I want to ask you: Is giving a passion
for you? Does it feel like an act of worship?
Does it bring you joy?

The way you answer those questions will
be an indication of where you are on your
journey from fear to joy. If you're anything
less than thrilled about giving generously,
then you've still got a ways to go.

THE ACCIDENTAL PHILANTHROPIST

Donald Rauer was not big on giving. As a
middle manager in a large manufacturing
company, he worked hard for every penny
he earned. For sixty hours a week he worked
magic in his department, turning his sweat
and blood into an elixir that motivated his
employees to be the company's perennial top
producers. As a twenty-five-year employee,
Donald was the backbone of his company's
productivity. He was a big believer in hard
work and fair pay. "There's no such thing
as a free lunch," he reminded his workers,
encouraging them to press on. And though
his team members were well compensated
for their success, it was no secret that they
earned it.

Donald had worked hard for everything he'd ever achieved. He was an undersized athlete in school, but he used hustle to land a football scholarship that paid most of his college expenses. The rest he earned working in a furniture store near the campus.

Like a curmudgeon from a Dickens novel, Donald was devoted to an economic philosophy that left little room for philanthropy.

Then one day Donald got a phone call that would change his life. Donald's sole living relative, Uncle Mike, had passed away after a long battle with emphysema. Donald was to receive a large sum of money. But that's not what changed his life. The executor of Uncle Mike's estate explained that the will included some rather unusual terms. Aware of his imminent death, Uncle Mike had set up a special foundation for half of his remaining assets; however, he had never decided on a beneficiary. The foundation now held close to a million dollars. Uncle Mike had always respected Donald's work ethic and judgment. So among his last wishes, he named Donald the trustee for his foundation. It was now up to Donald to decide how to distribute nearly one million dollars. And according to his uncle's wishes, he had twelve years in which to do it.

At first Donald tried to decline the assignment. Then he tried to ignore it. But it soon became obvious that the alternatives didn't make much sense. If he didn't allocate the funds, someone else would. And the least he could do was fulfill his uncle's wishes. So reluctantly, over the course of several months, he grew to accept his new role.

Keenly aware of the value of a dollar, Donald was a tenacious examiner of potential charities. With ruthless scrutiny he probed the operations of each candidate, looking for reasons to disqualify them. Eventually, Donald decided on a handful of organizations that even he found to be above reproach. As if conceding defeat, Donald finally began to allocate small sums to each one. What happened next was nothing short of a miracle.

In the months that followed, Donald began to receive reports on the work that was being accomplished by his reluctant gifts. Starving people were being fed. Abandoned children were receiving medical treatment. Itinerant farmers were taught to cultivate new crops to feed their villages.

Donald showed little interest at first. But his tough shell began to soften as he tracked the progress of these beneficiaries throughout the year. When urgent needs arose, Donald would often reallocate the foundation's resources to help out. Eventually, Donald began making annual treks so he could see his gifts at work firsthand. Before long, he was captivated.

To make a longer story short, Donald ended up taking semi-retirement from the plant in order to spend his summers as a volunteer relief worker. He found great pleasure fraternizing with the families he served. They sent letters and photos back and forth throughout the years. Eventually, Donald pioneered an exchange program that brought third-world families to the United States for a year of agricultural training. He often hosted the visitors in his own home.

For eight years, Donald's involvement in relief work escalated. With each passing year, he gave more of his time—and more of the foundation's money. Because of his enthusiasm, Donald fulfilled his uncle's wishes four years ahead of schedule. And when the money ran out, he did the unthinkable: He began transferring his own nest egg over to the foundation. To offset the depletion rate of his growing philanthropic efforts, Donald retitled a large portion of his estate to start an endowment fund for the foundation. To support his ongoing work, most of his salary and pension from the plant went directly into an operating account for the relief work. Donald worked about nine months at the plant every year, devoting the other three months completely to his newfound calling.

Donald finally retired from the plant at the age of seventy-one. He remained actively involved in the foundation's work for more than fifteen years after that. By the time he died, Donald's life was completely devoted to extending compassion to those in need. The most astonishing thing about Donald's life was not the impact he made through his gifts, but the impact the gifts made on him.

There was no fear in Donald's quest to give away his uncle's fortune. Because it was not his money, Donald wasn't worried about how spending the money would affect him personally. And without the influence of fear in his equation, Donald quickly became seduced by something we were all created to experience: the sheer joy of giving.

Imagine for a minute that you are

responsible for giving away someone else's money. You aren't allowed to spend it. You can only decide where it goes. When you think of it that way, it's not too hard to imagine finding pleasure in playing the philanthropist. Who wouldn't enjoy being a vital lifeline to those who truly needed it? What man or woman wouldn't sleep a little better knowing he or she had made a difference in the world?

And yet, when we have a proper perspective on our possessions, that's exactly the situation we find ourselves in. We have been given someone else's money. We have been given the opportunity to decide where it goes. And the only thing that stands between us and unbridled joy is embracing that reality and throwing ourselves into the work of Christian philanthropy.

A farmer doesn't acquire seed to consume it or to hoard it. He only decides where to plant it. And only when the seed has been irrevocably cast into the ground is a harvest returned. That's how joy is realized. If you've yet to find your beneficiaries in this world, you could be depriving yourself of a joy you were created to know. If fear keeps you from doing the rational thing with your seed—sowing—you are missing out on a harvest.

Maybe you're a reluctant philanthropist. But I'd like to encourage you with this thought: Just beyond the fear that is dampening your generosity awaits a harvest of joy. Past the foreboding peaks and lifeless valleys in your financial landscape are gentle, rolling fields of gold for those who will simply make the journey.

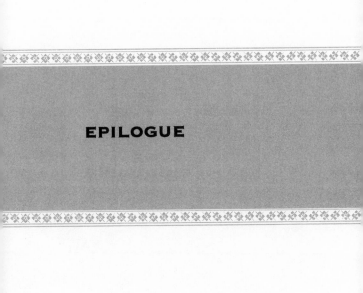

EPILOGUE

Jeremiah Clary sat back in the old oak rocking chair on his front porch. The morning sun was gleaming across an endless sea of golden, shimmering wheat in front of him. The early autumn air was crisp. A million sprinkles of dew made prisms out of rays of sunshine, giving the field a brilliant diamond coating. A light breeze gently stirred the wheat, creating rolling waves that looked like breakers of liquid gold washing ashore on Jeremiah's private beach. He smiled with delight.

Jeremiah thought back to six months earlier, during the days of torment and anxiety. He remembered the particular morning when it seemed life itself hung in the balance. He pictured himself huddled in that dusty, windblown barn, sitting atop the sacks of seed like a mother hen on full alert. Conditions had been perfect for planting at the end of the sowing season. But instead, Jeremiah was locked in the barn, the door held shut with mental bolts. It was a time when he struggled to keep a rational mind.

Since that time, many of Jeremiah's old friends had given up and moved on to California. Others had stayed, trying their hand at something besides farming. But Jeremiah had finally decided to put his hand to the plow one more time. Despite the fear of black blizzards, he mustered the courage to sow the fields with hope once again. And today was harvest day.

As Jeremiah mounted his Massey-Ferguson, he surveyed the richest crop on record in Harper County. It was like driving into a pot of gold. On that same harvest day, other farmers were living out their worst fears. Those who had cowered under the threat of dust storms without sowing were now bare-fielded and empty-handed. Jeremiah took a deep breath and set his leather hat around his brow like a crown of jewels. The flat horizon showed wheat as far as he could see. Fear was nowhere to be found.

ABOUT
GENEROUS GIVING

Studies show that U.S. Christians give proportionately less today than they did during the Great Depression.

Generous Giving is a nonprofit educational ministry that seeks to encourage givers of all income levels—as well as ministry leaders, pastors, teachers, and professional advisors—to fully understand and embrace what it means to live generously according to God's word and Christ's example. Generous Giving was launched in 2000 by the Maclellan Foundation, a fifty-year leader in Christian grant making, to stir a renewed commitment to generosity among Christians. *Our mission is to motivate followers of Christ toward greater biblical generosity.* We envision the hearts and minds of God's people transformed for revolutionary giving.

We offer an array of practical tools such as books, study guides, quarterly briefings, e-newsletters, and an exhaustive on-line library of news articles, statistics, Bible studies, streaming media, and Scriptures and sermons on generosity. We sponsor large and small gatherings, in a safe environment free from the pressure of solicitation, where givers can hear inspiring stories of men and women who have experienced financial freedom through the joy of giving.

We also host the Generous Giving Marketplace, a Web site that brings givers and ministry opportunities together (www.GGMarketplace.org). This is a one-of-a-kind classified listing of hundreds of funding opportunities posted by scores of Christian ministries.

See that you also excel in this grace of giving.
2 CORINTHIANS 8:7, NIV

For more information about Generous Giving, we invite you to contact:

Experience the Joy

Generous Giving, Inc.
One Fountain Square, Suite 501
Chattanooga, TN 37402
(423) 294-2399
www.GenerousGiving.org

More Generous Giving books from Tyndale . . .

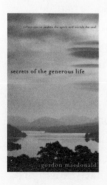

Secrets of the Generous Life
Gordon MacDonald
ISBN 0-8423-7385-3

In this book of inspiring and thought-provoking reflections, best-selling author Gordon MacDonald reveals the secrets of joyful, generous living and explains why a generous lifestyle is such an accurate measure of one's soul.

The Law of Rewards
Randy Alcorn
ISBN 0-8423-8106-6

From the best-selling author of
The Treasure Principle comes this
inspirational and motivational
book on God's incentive program.
Discover the source of true riches
and lasting joy as you refocus
your priorities and take a new look at the real route
to happiness.

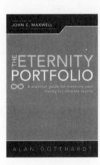

The Eternity Portfolio
Alan Gotthardt
ISBN 0-8423-8435-9

Respected CPA and financial
advisor Alan Gotthardt combines
biblical teaching with modern
investment-portfolio theory and
offers fresh, practical how-tos for
strategic, satisfying giving.